GAO

United States Government Accountability Office

Report to the Ranking Member, Committee on Health, Education, Labor, and Pensions, U.S. Senate

July 2012

PATIENT PROTECTION AND AFFORDABLE CARE ACT

Estimates of the Effect on the Prevalence of Employer-Sponsored Health Coverage

To access this report electronically, scan this QR Code.
Don't have a QR code reader? Several are available for free online.

GAO-12-768

Highlights of GAO-12-768, a report to the Ranking Member, Committee on Health, Education, Labor, and Pensions, U.S. Senate

July 2012

PATIENT PROTECTION AND AFFORDABLE CARE ACT

Estimates of the Effect on the Prevalence of Employer-Sponsored Health Coverage

Why GAO Did This Study

The share of employers offering health coverage has generally declined in the last decade. Researchers believe that certain provisions of PPACA could affect employers' future willingness to offer health coverage, such as the availability of subsidized coverage through new health insurance marketplaces called "exchanges" and an "individual mandate," which will require most people to obtain health coverage or pay a tax penalty. Certain PPACA provisions are scheduled to take effect in 2014. Researchers have provided various estimates of the effect PPACA may have on employer-sponsored coverage.

GAO was asked to review the research on this topic. GAO examined (1) estimates of the effect of PPACA on the extent of employer-sponsored coverage; (2) factors that may contribute to the variation in estimates; and (3) how estimates of coverage vary by the types of employers and employees that may be affected, as well as other changes employers may be considering to the health benefits they offer. GAO reviewed studies published from January 1, 2009, through March 30, 2012 containing an original numerical estimate of the prevalence of employer-sponsored coverage at the national level. These included 5 microsimulation models and 19 employer surveys. Microsimulation models can systematically estimate the combined effects of multiple PPACA provisions in terms of both gains and losses of coverage; their results are based on multiple data sets and assumptions. Surveys reflect employer perspectives; they have limits as a predictive tool in part based on varied survey methodologies and respondent knowledge of PPACA.

View GAO-12-768. For more information, contact John E.Dicken at (202) 512-7114 or dickenj@gao.gov.

What GAO Found

The five studies GAO reviewed that used microsimulation models to estimate the effects of the Patient Protection and Affordable Care Act (PPACA) on employer-sponsored coverage generally predicted little change in prevalence in the near term, while results of employer surveys varied more widely. The five microsimulation study estimates ranged from a net decrease of 2.5 percent to a net increase of 2.7 percent in the total number of individuals with employer-sponsored coverage within the first 2 years of implementation of key PPACA provisions, affecting up to about 4 million individuals. Two of these studies also indicated that the majority of individuals losing employer-sponsored coverage would transition to other sources of coverage. In contrast to the microsimulation studies, which estimate the net effect on individuals, most employer surveys measure the percentage of employers that may drop coverage in response to PPACA. Among the 19 surveys, 16 reported estimates of employers dropping coverage for all employee types. Among these 16, 11 indicated that 10 percent or fewer employers were likely to drop coverage in the near term, but estimates ranged from 2 to 20 percent. Most surveys were of employers currently offering coverage and therefore did not also address whether other employers may begin to offer coverage in response to PPACA; however, 3 that did found that between 1 and 28 percent would begin offering coverage as a result of PPACA. Longer-term predictions of prevalence of employer-sponsored coverage were fewer and more uncertain, and four microsimulation studies estimated that from about 2 million to 6 million fewer individuals would have employer-sponsored coverage in the absence of the individual mandate compared to with the mandate.

Differences in key assumptions and consideration of PPACA provisions likely contributed to some variation among estimates from the five microsimulation studies and the 16 employer surveys. Variation among the microsimulation studies may have stemmed from differences in assumptions about employer and employee decision making, the time frames of the estimates, and assessments of potential compliance with the individual mandate. Variation among the employer surveys may be related to differences in survey sampling techniques, the number and types of employer respondents, and the framing of survey questions. For example, some surveys used a random sampling methodology, allowing their results to be generalized across all employers, while others did not. Also, some referred to specific PPACA provisions or provided specific information about provisions to respondents, while others did not.

Some of the 19 employer surveys indicated that PPACA may have a larger effect on small employers and certain populations and may prompt some employers to change benefit designs. For example, 4 surveys found that smaller employers were more likely than other employers to stop offering health coverage in response to PPACA, and 5 found that employers in general were more likely to drop coverage for retirees than for all employees. Nine surveys also indicated that employers are considering key changes to benefit design, some of which may result in greater employee cost for health coverage.

GAO provided a draft of this report to two researchers with expertise in employee health benefits issues. The experts agreed with GAO's report and provided technical comments, which were incorporated as appropriate.

United States Government Accountability Office

Contents

Letter		1
	Background	5
	Microsimulation Models Predicted Little Near-Term Change in Employer-Sponsored Coverage, but Other Studies and Employer Surveys Varied More Widely	10
	Differences in Key Assumptions and Consideration of PPACA Provisions Likely Contributed to Variation in Estimates among Studies Using Similar Techniques	18
	Employer Surveys Suggest That PPACA May Have a Larger Effect on Small Employers and Certain Employee Populations and Prompt Some Employers to Change Benefit Designs	25
	External Comments	28
Appendix I	Studies Reviewed by GAO	30
Appendix II	GAO Contact and Staff Acknowledgments	36
Table		
	Table 1: Employer Survey Results regarding Percentage of Employers Likely to Drop Coverage for Employees in the Near Term	14
Figures		
	Figure 1: Microsimulation Model Predictions of Near-Term Changes in Employer-Sponsored Coverage as a Result of PPACA	11
	Figure 2: Effect of PPACA on Employer-Sponsored Coverage with and without the Individual Mandate	17

Abbreviations

CBO	Congressional Budget Office
CDHP	Consumer-Directed Health Plan
CMS	Centers for Medicare & Medicaid Services
CPS	Current Population Survey
EBRI	Employee Benefit Research Institute
EPI	Employment Policies Institute
HCERA	Health Care and Education Reconciliation Act of 2010
HDHP	High Deductible Health Plan
HRET	Health Research & Educational Trust
IFEBP	International Foundation of Employee Benefit Plans
MBGH	Midwest Business Group on Health
MEPS	Medical Expenditure Panel Survey
NFIB	National Federation of Independent Business
PPACA	Patient Protection and Affordable Care Act
RWJF	Robert Wood Johnson Foundation
SHOP	Small Business Health Options Program
SIPP	Survey of Income and Program Participation

This is a work of the U.S. government and is not subject to copyright protection in the United States. The published product may be reproduced and distributed in its entirety without further permission from GAO. However, because this work may contain copyrighted images or other material, permission from the copyright holder may be necessary if you wish to reproduce this material separately.

United States Government Accountability Office
Washington, DC 20548

July 13, 2012

The Honorable Michael B. Enzi
Ranking Member
Committee on Health, Education, Labor, and Pensions
United States Senate

Dear Senator Enzi:

Employer-sponsored health coverage is the leading source of health coverage in the United States and was provided to more than 156 million Americans under age 65 (about 59 percent) in 2010.[1] Nearly all large employers and more than half of small employers offer health coverage to their employees, in part as a means of recruiting and retaining employees.[2] Most employees participate in employer-sponsored coverage when it is available,[3] in part because employers typically subsidize a large share of employees' premiums, these premium contributions are generally excluded from taxable income, and employees may lack other affordable health coverage options.[4] The proportion of employers offering health coverage has declined in the last decade—from

---

[1] See Paul Fronstin, "Sources of Health Insurance and Characteristics of the Uninsured: Analysis of the March 2011 Current Population Survey," *Employee Benefit Research Institute Issue Brief*, no. 362 (2011).

[2] See Kaiser Family Foundation and Health Research & Education Trust (HRET), *Employer Health Benefits 2011 Annual Survey* (Menlo Park, Calif., and Chicago, Ill.: September 2011). In this report, large employers are defined as those with 200 or more employees, while small employers are those with 3 to 199 employees.

[3] M. W. Stanton and M. K. Rutherford, *Employer-Sponsored Health Insurance: Trends in Cost and Access*, a report prepared for the Agency for Healthcare Research and Quality, Research in Action Issue 17, AHRQ Pub. No. 04-0085 (Rockville, Md.: 2004).

[4] Individual health coverage purchased directly through an insurer in the individual market is typically more expensive than comparable employer-sponsored coverage. For example, the average individual premium for single coverage in 2010 was $2,580 compared to the average employee contribution for employer-sponsored single coverage of about $900. Further, unlike employer-sponsored coverage, insurers in the individual markets of most states may also restrict eligibility for individual coverage based on a person's health status or pre-existing heath conditions.

68 percent of all employers in 2001 to 60 percent in 2011, with most of the decline occurring by 2005.[5]

The Patient Protection and Affordable Care Act (PPACA), enacted in March 2010,[6] contains a number of provisions that some researchers of employer-sponsored health coverage indicate may affect employers' willingness to offer health coverage to their employees.[7] Researchers believe some provisions—such as financial penalties that certain employers with at least 50 full-time equivalent employees may face if they do not offer health coverage or if they offer coverage that does not meet certain minimum requirements, and an "individual mandate," which will require most people to obtain health coverage or pay a tax penalty—may encourage employers to continue offering or newly offer health coverage. However, some researchers believe certain PPACA provisions that result in coverage from other sources—such as an expanded Medicaid program and subsidized coverage for certain individuals who purchase coverage through new health insurance marketplaces called "exchanges"—may discourage employers from offering coverage. Recent studies have predicted employers' responses to PPACA in terms of offering coverage once key PPACA provisions are in effect. You requested that we review existing research on the potential effect of PPACA on the prevalence of employer-sponsored coverage. Based on this request, we examined

1. estimates of the effect of PPACA on the prevalence of employer-sponsored health coverage, including the number of individuals with employer-sponsored coverage and the proportion of employers that would offer coverage to their employees;

2. the factors that may contribute to varying estimates; and

3. how estimates vary by the types of employers and employees that may be affected, as well as other changes employers may be considering to the health benefits they offer.

---

[5]See Kaiser Family Foundation and HRET, *2011 Annual Survey*.

[6]Pub. L. No. 111-148, 124 Stat. 119 (2010), as amended by the Health Care and Education Reconciliation Act of 2010 (HCERA), Pub. L. No. 111-152, 124 Stat. 1029. For purposes of this report, references to PPACA include the amendments made by HCERA.

[7]Certain PPACA provisions are scheduled to take effect in 2014.

To conduct this work, we identified and reviewed 27 studies, published from January 1, 2009, through March 30, 2012,[8] which fell into three broad study types—5 based on microsimulation models,[9] 3 based on other analytic approaches, and 19 based on employer surveys.[10] We included in our report only those studies from our review that provided an original numerical estimate at the national level of the likely prevalence of, or changes to, rates of employer-sponsored health coverage as a result of PPACA. To identify these studies, we conducted a review of research databases using relevant search terms. We also identified studies available online from research organizations, consulting firms, and other relevant websites. In addition, we included studies that met our criteria from a June 2011 report by Avalere Health, a health care consulting firm. This report provided a comprehensive review of studies published by that time, comparing estimates of the effect of PPACA on employer-sponsored health coverage.[11] We also reviewed the bibliographies of the selected studies for additional studies that met our criteria. (See app. I for a complete list of these studies.)

---

[8]We included studies published during or subsequent to 2009 because key elements of PPACA were being considered by Congress at this time.

[9]Microsimulation models are statistical models that have been used since the 1950s to predict behavioral responses to changes in economic and social policies. They are commonly used by government agencies such as the Department of Labor and the Congressional Budget Office to model the effects of policies, programs, and proposed legislation. The studies we reviewed used models that attempted to predict the behavior of employees and employers in response to changes in health policy brought about by PPACA. To simulate likely responses, these models rely on a variety of elements, including economic theory, national survey data, and existing empirical evidence from related or smaller-scale policy changes, such as prior changes in Medicaid eligibility and state insurance reform efforts.

[10]Where authors published more recent studies containing updated estimates from those in their prior studies, we primarily cited the most recent estimates. Multiple microsimulation studies conducted by the same organization were counted as one study for our purposes because they used the same proprietary microsimulation model (despite changing certain modeling assumptions and, in some cases, using updated data in more recent studies). Similarly, employer surveys conducted by the same firm in multiple years were counted as one study because the newer surveys generally updated findings from the previous survey. However, we reviewed each of the surveys and microsimulation models for the report, and where appropriate, we cite results of older studies that were not updated in newer studies.

[11]See Avalere Health LLC, *The Affordable Care Act's Impact on Employer-Sponsored Insurance: A Look At the Microsimulation Models and Other Analyses* (Washington, D.C.: 2011).

To examine estimates of the effect of PPACA on the prevalence of employer-sponsored health coverage, we summarized information from our review of studies. From the microsimulation studies and studies using other analytic approaches, we summarized estimates of net changes in the number of individuals who may be affected by employers dropping, as well as newly offering, coverage as a result of PPACA. We did not summarize other changes employers may make to employee compensation packages to remain competitive in the labor force, such as providing compensation for lost coverage to enable employees to purchase coverage elsewhere. From employer surveys, we summarized the percentage of surveyed employers likely to drop employer-sponsored coverage as a result of PPACA.[12] To examine the factors that could account for varying estimates, we reviewed the key assumptions and methods used in the studies we identified. In particular, to evaluate the studies based on microsimulation models and other analytic approaches, we examined underlying key assumptions that the studies used when modeling employer and employee behavior in making decisions about health coverage, as well as assumptions about the effectiveness of relevant PPACA provisions and how the provisions might be implemented. We examined the authors' own assessments of their study methods as well as publicly available assessments by other researchers. To evaluate the employer surveys, we used publicly available information about the survey instrument, methodology, sample size, and the response rate. Information on employer response rates—which can be an important measure of the ability to generalize survey results beyond the employers surveyed—was not publicly available for most surveys. We did not interview the study authors. To examine how estimates varied by the types of employers and employees that may be affected, we summarized information from the employer surveys that provided estimates by the type of employer and employees. We also summarized other predicted changes in employer-sponsored coverage, such as changes in benefit design.[13]

---

[12]Most employer surveys did not examine the extent to which employers may newly offer coverage as a result of PPACA.

[13]Most microsimulation studies and studies using other analytic approaches that we reviewed did not provide estimates of the prevalence of employer-sponsored coverage by type of employer or employee, or estimates of other changes in benefit design.

We conducted this performance audit from February 2012 through July 2012 in accordance with generally accepted government auditing standards. Those standards require that we plan and perform the audit to obtain sufficient, appropriate evidence to provide a reasonable basis for our findings and conclusions based on our audit objectives. We believe that the evidence obtained provides a reasonable basis for our findings and conclusions based on our audit objectives.

Background

Employer-sponsored health coverage is the leading source of health coverage in the United States. In 2010, 59 percent of Americans under age 65 received health coverage through employer-sponsored group health plans, and an additional 7 percent received coverage through health coverage purchased directly from health insurers in the individual market.[14] Employers may provide coverage either by purchasing coverage from a health insurer (fully insured plans) or by funding their own health coverage (self-insured plans). Small employers typically offer fully insured plans, while large employers are more likely to be self-insured.[15] Small employers are also less likely to offer their employees health coverage compared to large employers, citing the cost of coverage as a key reason.[16] Additionally, firms with more high-wage workers are more likely to offer coverage to their employees than those with more low-wage workers. Rates of employer-sponsored health coverage have declined in the last decade—from 68 percent in 2001 to 60 percent in 2011. Most of this decline occurred by 2005 and was driven primarily by a

---

[14]Another 22 percent of Americans under age 65 received coverage through public programs such as Medicare and Medicaid, and an additional 19 percent were uninsured. Percentages do not sum to 100 because estimates of coverage types are not mutually exclusive and individuals can have more than one type of coverage during the year. See Fronstin, "Sources of Health Insurance and Characteristics of the Uninsured."

[15]Self-insured employee health benefit plans are not subject to state insurance regulations or to certain requirements in PPACA that apply to fully insured plans—for example, required coverage of certain "essential" health benefits. See 29 U.S.C. § 1144 (certain employee benefit plans not subject to state laws); 42 U.S.C. §§ 18021, 18022 (as added by Pub. L. No. 111-148, §§ 1301, 1302, 124 Stat. 162,163) (certain employee benefit plans excluded from definition of "health plan" and requirement to provide essential health benefits under PPACA).

[16]In 2011, almost all (99 percent) of large employers (those with 200 or more workers) offered health coverage, compared to 59 percent of small employers (those with 3 to 199 workers). In the small employer category, 48 percent of the smallest employers (those with 3 to 9 workers) offered health coverage. See Kaiser Family Foundation and HRET, *2011 Annual Survey*.

decline in the number of very small employers with three to nine employees offering health coverage. In addition, employee participation in employer-sponsored coverage has also decreased—from 70 percent in 2001 to 65 percent in 2011, in part because of a decline in employee eligibility for the coverage.[17] Further, employees' share of the cost of coverage is increasing faster than employers' share—the employee contribution to the average annual premium for family coverage increased 131 percent from 2001 to 2011 compared to a 108 percent increase in the employer contribution for the same time period.[18]

PPACA contains a number of provisions that may affect whether employers offer health coverage. These provisions include

- an "individual mandate," or the requirement that individuals—subject to certain exceptions—obtain minimum essential health coverage or pay a tax penalty starting in 2014;

- the establishment of health insurance exchanges in 2014— essentially, health insurance marketplaces in which individuals and small businesses can compare, select, and purchase health coverage from among participating carriers;

- health insurance market reforms including a requirement that prevents health plans and insurers in the individual and small group markets from denying coverage or charging higher premiums because of pre-existing conditions or medical history, and that limits the extent to which premiums may vary;[19]

---

[17] Employees may not be eligible for employer-sponsored coverage because they work on a part-time or temporary basis, or have not completed a required waiting period. Eligible employees may choose not to participate for several reasons, including the non-affordability of the coverage, or because they have coverage through other sources. See Paul Fronstin, "Employment-Based Health Benefits: Trends in Access and Coverage 1997–2010," *Employee Benefit Research Institute Issue Brief*, no. 370 (2012).

[18] See Kaiser Family Foundation and HRET, *2011 Annual Survey*.

[19] For example, insurers may vary premiums based on factors such as age, but not on health status, and the premiums may vary by no more than a 3 to 1 ratio for adults, meaning that the rate for the oldest person would be no more than three times higher than for the youngest person.

- premium subsidies—which provide sliding scale tax credits starting in 2014 to limit premium costs for individuals and families with incomes up to 400 percent of the federal poverty level—for purchasing individual coverage through an exchange;

- penalties for certain large employers that do not offer qualified health coverage and have at least one full-time employee receiving a subsidy (in the form of a premium tax credit or cost-sharing reduction) in a plan offered through an exchange starting in 2014, or for certain large employers that provide access to coverage but do not meet certain requirements for affordability;[20]

- tax credits for certain small businesses toward a share of their employee health coverage beginning in 2010;

- a 40 percent excise tax on certain employer-sponsored health plans whose costs exceed a certain threshold in 2018;[21] and

- a state Medicaid expansion effective in 2014 for individuals who are under 65 years old, have incomes at or below 133 percent of the federal poverty level, and meet other specified criteria.[22]

Researchers have used various types of studies to predict the effect of PPACA on employer-sponsored health insurance, including microsimulation models, other analytic approaches, and employer surveys. Microsimulation models—commonly used statistical models—generally use published survey data to construct a base data set of

---

[20]IRS has proposed establishing a future safe harbor in this context such that the threshold would be established at 9.5 percent of an employee's household income. Request for Comments on Health Coverage Affordability Safe Harbor for Employers, Treasury Notice 2011-73.

[21]Threshold amounts in 2018 are $10,200 for single coverage and $27,500 for nonsingle coverage. These amounts will be indexed for inflation in subsequent years. See 26 U.S.C. § 4980I, as added by Pub. L. No. 111-148, §§ 9001, 10901, 124 Stat. 847, 1015 and Pub. L. No. 111-152, § 1401, 124 Stat. 1059.

[22]The U.S. Supreme Court has ruled that states may choose not to expand Medicaid coverage to this group of individuals and forgo only the federal matching funds associated with such expanded coverage. See *National Federation of Independent Business, et al., vs. Sebelius, Sec. of Health and Human Services, et al.*, No. 11-393 (U.S. June 28, 2012). Estimates of Medicaid enrollment used in studies cited in this report were made prior to the Supreme Court decision and are therefore likely to assume expanded Medicaid participation under PPACA by all states.

individuals, families, and employers, and then attempt to predict responses to public policy changes by drawing from the best available evidence in health economics literature and, in some cases, existing empirical evidence from related or smaller-scale policy changes (such as prior changes in Medicaid eligibility and state insurance reform efforts). The models systematically estimate the combined effect of multiple provisions in legislation, such as PPACA, based on this previous research and empirical data. For example, with respect to PPACA, models can provide an estimate of employer-sponsored coverage that considers both the number of employers that may discontinue offering coverage and the number that may begin to offer coverage. Models can also incorporate into their analyses estimates of the number of employees who may take up or refuse offers of such coverage. Model limitations include their dependence upon multiple types of data from multiple sources of varying quality and that they must rely on many assumptions.[23] The impact of past policy changes also may not necessarily be predictive of the impact of future changes, and there is little information available with which to assess the validity of their projections.[24] Studies we reviewed using other analytic approaches to model behavior in response to policy changes

---

[23]Researchers may include analyses that test the sensitivity of their results to changes in various assumptions.

[24]Some researchers have noted that predictions of employer responses to PPACA in the microsimulation studies are generally consistent with employer responses to health care reform in Massachusetts that contained certain provisions similar to PPACA, including an individual mandate, exchanges, employer penalties, and subsidies for low-income individuals. Others suggest that the experience in Massachusetts cannot be generalized nationally because of differences between health reform provisions in that state and PPACA. For example, employer penalties do not apply to self-insured employers in Massachusetts, but they do apply under PPACA. Further, one researcher noted that the imposition of employer penalties in Massachusetts (under which employers not offering coverage would pay a share of uncompensated care costs for their employees) might provide a greater incentive for employers to offer coverage than the employer penalty under PPACA. The researcher also noted that because Massachusetts had one of the highest rates of insurance coverage in the country prior to the implementation of state health reform, its resulting response to health reform may differ from those of other states.

varied in their methods, ranging from a cost-benefit comparison to an analysis that used survey data and economic theory to predict behavior.[25]

Employer surveys have also been cited to illustrate the potential impact of PPACA on employer health benefits. Unlike microsimulation models, surveys have the advantage of reflecting the actual, current perspectives of employers, and they can also assess how employers' behavior may be affected by the actions of other employers of similar size and industry. However, they have limitations as a predictive tool. For example, most surveys relating to PPACA asked respondents about employers' likelihood of dropping coverage, rather than the likelihood of newly offering coverage as a result of PPACA or the number of employees that may take up or refuse such coverage. Thus, they may not illustrate the net effect of PPACA on employer-sponsored coverage. Further, the validity of their results may be limited by the knowledge of survey respondents. Experts have noted that employer surveys tend to be answered by human resource officials with varying levels of knowledge about PPACA. In addition, researchers note that survey responses do not require careful analysis or extensive deliberation and have no consequences for the responders. Therefore, surveys are more limited in their ability to systematically assess the combined effect of multiple PPACA provisions—that is, they cannot ensure that respondents consider (or have the ability to consider) all of the relevant provisions when deciding how to respond. Moreover, the results of the sample of employers surveyed may not always be generalizable to all employers, depending on the number of respondents and other aspects of the survey methodology.

---

[25]The analysis that used survey data and economic theory to predict behavior was similar in some respects to a microsimulation model. However, its purpose was not to estimate the effects of PPACA on employer-sponsored coverage per se, but rather to illustrate how these estimates could change under varying assumptions about the cost of health insurance. Unlike the microsimulation models, it focused on a subset of the working population and did not consider all of PPACA's provisions.

Microsimulation Models Predicted Little Near-Term Change in Employer-Sponsored Coverage, but Other Studies and Employer Surveys Varied More Widely

Microsimulation studies generally predicted little change in employer-sponsored health coverage in the near term, but results of studies using other analytic approaches and employer surveys varied more widely. Few studies provided longer-term predictions of the prevalence of employer-sponsored coverage, and those that did so expressed uncertainty about their estimates. Microsimulation studies that examined the effect of the individual mandate estimated that more people would have employer-sponsored coverage with the mandate in place compared to without the mandate.

Microsimulation Studies Predicted Small Near-Term Changes to Employer-Sponsored Coverage

Among the five microsimulation studies we reviewed, estimates of PPACA's net effect on changes in the rates of employer-sponsored coverage ranged in the near term from a decrease of 2.5 percent to an increase of 2.7 percent in the number of individuals with coverage.[26] In particular, three projected an increase in the number of individuals with coverage. The Centers for Medicare & Medicaid (CMS) estimated a net increase of about 0.1 percent (200,000 individuals), and the studies by the RAND Corporation (RAND) and the Urban Institute/Robert Wood Johnson Foundation (RWJF) each projected a net increase of 2.7 percent affecting about 4 million individuals. The remaining two studies projected a decrease: the Congressional Budget Office (CBO) projected a 2.5 percent net decrease affecting about 4 million individuals, while The Lewin Group projected a net decrease of 1.6 percent affecting about 2 million individuals. (See fig. 1.)

---

[26] We consider effects likely to take place within 2 years of the implementation of a provision of PPACA to be in the "near term" and those likely to take place over a longer period to be "long term." Some studies assessed the effects of PPACA as if key provisions were implemented in or by a certain year, such as 2011. We consider these studies to be examining the near-term effects of PPACA. Other studies assessed the effects of PPACA over a range of years, incorporating provision phase-in dates established in the legislation; for these studies, we consider the estimates up to 2016 to be near term because key provisions are scheduled to take effect in 2014. In each study, predicted changes are estimated as compared to a baseline level of coverage in a given year without implementation of PPACA.

Figure 1: Microsimulation Model Predictions of Near-Term Changes in Employer-Sponsored Coverage as a Result of PPACA

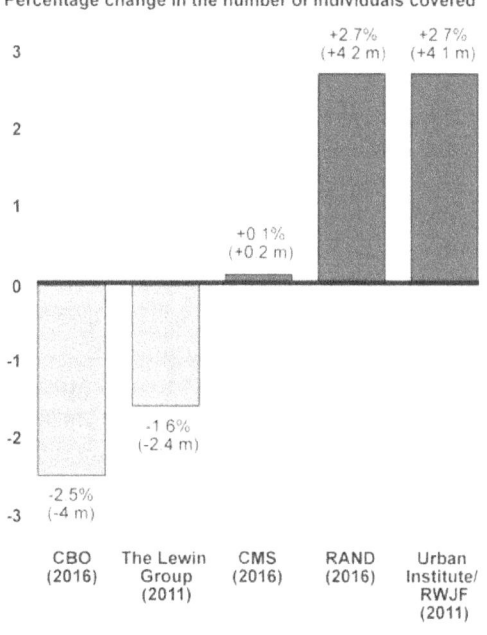

Author

Source: GAO analysis of data from CBO, The Lewin Group, CMS, RAND, and the Urban Institute/RWJF.

Notes: For full citations of studies, see app. I.

Predicted changes are estimated as compared to predicted baseline coverage in a given year without PPACA. The estimates are for different time frames: the CBO, CMS, and RAND estimates are for 2016, and The Lewin Group and Urban Institute/RWJF estimates are for 2011 (assuming implementation of key PPACA provisions). Since baseline estimates of coverage without PPACA may differ between models, the number of individuals with employer-sponsored coverage after implementation of PPACA may vary despite similar percentage changes.

Two of the studies also indicated that the majority of individuals who lose employer-sponsored coverage would transition to other sources of coverage. For example, the RAND study indicated that out of the 6.5 million individuals it projected to lose employer-sponsored coverage after implementation of PPACA, 1.9 million would enroll in individual coverage through an exchange and 3.5 million would enroll in Medicaid. The remaining 1.1 million individuals would become uninsured.[27]

Estimates from Studies Using Other Analytic Approaches Varied More Widely

Estimates from the three studies we reviewed that used other analytic approaches varied more widely than those from the microsimulation models. Two of the three studies predicted small near-term changes in the number of individuals with employer-sponsored coverage. One of the studies, published by the Employment Policies Institute (EPI), used a modeling approach that predicted behavioral responses of all workers in a nationally representative sample to three main provisions of PPACA. This study projected a net increase of about 6 percent, or 4 million, in the number of individuals with employer-sponsored coverage.[28] Another study by Booz & Company Inc. that used a combination of surveys, interviews, focus groups, and modeling projected a net decrease of 2 to 3 percent, or from 3 million to 4 million individuals.[29] The third study, conducted by the American Action Forum, used a decision-making model based on cost-benefit comparisons to project a larger decrease of up to 35 million in the number of people with employer-sponsored coverage.[30] However, this study did not consider whether employers may newly offer coverage or estimate the number of individuals that would be newly covered as a result.

---

[27]Although this study indicated that 6.5 million individuals would lose employer-sponsored coverage after implementation of PPACA, it also found that 10.7 million individuals would be newly covered, resulting in a net gain of 4.2 million individuals with employer-sponsored coverage.

[28]This estimate was for 2008, assuming that three key PPACA provisions were implemented in that year. See R. V. Burkhauser, S. Lyons, and K. Simon, *An Offer You Can't Refuse: Estimating the Coverage Effects of the 2010 Affordable Care Act*, (Washington, D.C.: Employment Policies Institute, July 2011).

[29]This estimate was for 2016 compared to coverage without PPACA in 2009. See G. D. Ahlquist, P. F. Borromeo, and S. B. Saxena, *The Future of Health Insurance: Demise of Employer-Sponsored Coverage Greatly Exaggerated*, Booz & Company Inc. (2011).

[30]This estimate was for 2014. See D. Holtz-Eakin and C. Smith, *Labor Markets and Health Care Reform: New Results*, American Action Forum (2010).

Employer Surveys Varied Widely in Their Estimates of PPACA's Effect on Employer-Sponsored Coverage

Employer surveys varied widely in their estimates of employers' responses to PPACA. Sixteen of the 19 surveys we reviewed reported estimates of employers dropping coverage for employees in general (rather than only for certain types of employees).[31] Among these 16 surveys, 11 indicated that 10 percent or fewer of employers were likely to drop coverage in the near term, and 5 indicated that from 11 to 20 percent were likely to drop coverage in the near term.[32] The estimates ranged from 2 to 20 percent across these 16 surveys. (See table 1.) Because these surveys were typically of employers currently offering coverage, most did not reflect the number of employers that may be likely to begin offering coverage under PPACA.

---

[31]We excluded 3 of the 19 total surveys from this analysis. One survey did not include an estimate of employers dropping coverage but only provided an estimate of small employers newly offering coverage as a result of PPACA. See Kaiser Family Foundation and HRET, *2011 Annual Survey*. The remaining 2 surveys included estimates only for retired, but not all, employees. See Aon Hewitt, *Employer Reaction to Health Care Reform: Retiree Strategy Survey, 2011* (Lincolnshire, Ill.: 2011), and National Business Group on Health, *Large Employers' 2011 Health Plan Design Changes* (Washington, D.C.: 2010).

[32]"Likely" responses include employers that stated they were "likely," "definitely likely," or "very likely" to drop coverage, or were "seriously considering" dropping coverage. For two surveys (Benfield Research and International Foundation of Employee Benefit Plans), "likely" responses included those "considering" dropping coverage because there was no other affirmative response available. Surveys generally specified only near-term time frames. One survey did not separate out "likely" from "somewhat likely" responses.

Table 1: Employer Survey Results regarding Percentage of Employers Likely to Drop Coverage for Employees in the Near Term

Organization	Size of employers surveyed	Percentage of employers likely to drop coverage in the near term
National Federation of Independent Business	Small (50 or fewer employees)	2
Towers Watson	Midsize and large: from 2,000 to 10,000+ employees	2
International Foundation of Employee Benefit Plans (IFEBP)	Small and large employers from IFEBP membership: employers with annual revenues ranging from less than $1 million to over $1 billion	3
Benfield Research	Jumbo (5,000+) employees only	4
Mercer	All sizes: 10+ employees	5
Willis	All sizes. Fewer than 500 employees, 25 percent; 500 to 4,999 employees, 43 percent; and 5,000+ employees, 33 percent	5
HR Policy Association	Large employers (not defined) drawn from the organization's membership	6
Midwest Business Group on Health	58 percent were employers with 500+ employees; 25 percent had 50 to 500 employees	6
PricewaterhouseCoopers	All employers	7
Market Strategies International	All sizes from at least 2 employees	9
McKinsey & Co.	All sizes from <20 employees to >10,000 employees	9
GfK Custom Research North America	N/A	12
Ceridian	N/A	19
Lockton Companies	N/A	19
Fidelity Investments	N/A	20
HighRoads	N/A	20

Source: GAO analysis of employer surveys.

Notes: "Likely" responses include employers that stated they were "likely," "definitely likely," or "very likely" to drop coverage, or were "seriously considering" dropping coverage. For two surveys (Benfield Research and IFEBP), "likely" responses included those "considering" dropping coverage because there was no other affirmative response available. Near term is defined as generally within 2 years of implementation of key PPACA provisions. Surveys are for different time periods.

A higher proportion of employers indicated that they were "somewhat likely" to drop coverage, among the 6 surveys that also provided this response option.[33] Among these surveys, 2 (the National Federation of

---

[33] The Mercer survey provided a choice of "very likely" and "likely" responses. We included the "very likely" response in the count of the 16 surveys in fig. 1, and the "likely" response in this count of 6 surveys with "somewhat likely" responses.

Independent Businesses (NFIB) and Towers Watson) indicated that 10 percent or fewer of employers were "somewhat likely" to drop coverage, 2 surveys (Willis and Mercer) indicated that 11 to 20 percent of employers had such plans, and the remaining 2 surveys (McKinsey & Co. (McKinsey) and PricewaterhouseCoopers) indicated that over 20 percent had such plans. In addition, two surveys asked respondents how their decisions to drop or offer coverage may be affected by other employers' actions. In one survey 78 percent of employers indicated that they were planning to follow the lead of other employers. In the other survey 25 percent of employers indicated that it would have a "major impact" on their decision if "one or a few large, bellwether employers" or one of their major competitors dropped coverage for a majority or all of their employees.

Three of the 16 surveys that also examined employer plans to newly offer coverage as a result of PPACA indicated that from 1 and 28 percent of employers were likely to do so. The NFIB survey indicated that about 1 percent of the employers surveyed were likely to begin offering coverage as a result of PPACA; the McKinsey survey indicated that 13 percent of employers with 2 to 49 employees, and 14 percent of employers with 50 to 499 employees, were likely to begin offering coverage. In addition, the Kaiser Family Foundation/Health Research & Educational Trust survey that examined employer plans to only newly offer (but not drop) coverage indicated that 15 percent of small employers (fewer than 50 employees) that did not offer health coverage and were aware of the small business tax credit were planning to add coverage as a result of it;[34] and the Market Strategies International survey indicated that 28 percent of employers not offering health coverage would begin to do so.

Estimates of Longer-Term Effects of PPACA on Employer-Sponsored Coverage Were Fewer and Less Certain

Among the studies we reviewed, only two microsimulation studies examined the longer-term effects of PPACA on employer-sponsored coverage. CMS projected that the number of individuals with employer-sponsored coverage would decrease by approximately 1 percent relative to estimates without PPACA in each year from 2017 through 2019, and that this annual gap would accelerate after that as a result of the high-

---

[34]GAO recently reported on the use of the small business tax credit under PPACA. See GAO, *Small Employer Health Tax Credit: Factors Contributing to Low Use and Complexity*, GAO-12-549 (Washington, D.C.: May 14, 2012).

cost plan excise tax. CBO projected a drop of about 3 percent, slightly larger than its near-term estimate, in employer-sponsored coverage in each year from 2017 through 2019, relative to estimates without PPACA in each year, and projected that this annual gap would decrease thereafter. The studies also noted that there is a large amount of uncertainty regarding how employers and employees will respond to policy changes as sweeping and complex as those included in PPACA, and some researchers indicated that long-term predictions of the effects of PPACA are particularly uncertain.

Studies Predicted Larger Decreases in Employer-Sponsored Coverage without the Individual Mandate

Four of the five microsimulation studies examined the effect of the individual mandate and predicted that fewer individuals would have employer-sponsored coverage without the mandate as compared to with the mandate. These studies separately estimated the effect of PPACA both with and without the individual mandate. The estimates ranged from about 2 million to 6 million fewer people covered without the mandate compared to with the mandate. (See fig. 2.)

Figure 2: Effect of PPACA on Employer-Sponsored Coverage with and without the Individual Mandate

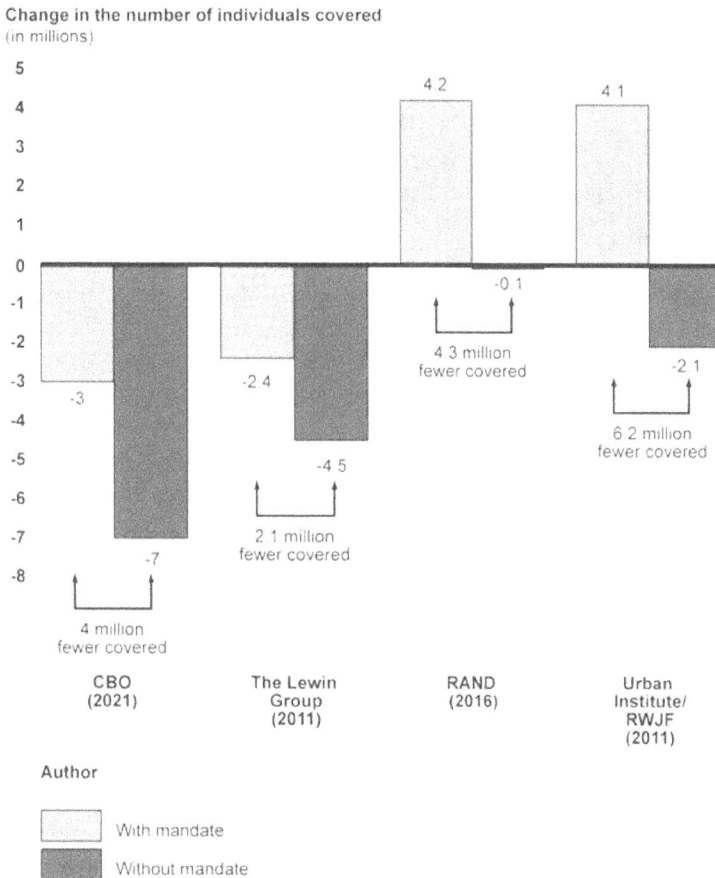

Notes: The CBO estimate of the effect of PPACA with the mandate noted here (-3 million) differs from the estimate noted in fig. 1 (-4 million) because CBO's analysis of the effect of eliminating the individual mandate used the agency's 2010, rather than its 2012, projections, and predicted PPACA's effect in 2021, rather than 2016. In each study, predicted changes are estimated as compared to a baseline level of coverage in a given year without implementation of PPACA. The estimates presented in this figure are for different time frames: the CBO estimate is for 2021, the RAND estimates are for 2016, and The Lewin Group and Urban Institute/RWJF estimates are for 2011 (assuming implementation of key PPACA provisions).

Differences in Key Assumptions and Consideration of PPACA Provisions Likely Contributed to Variation in Estimates among Studies Using Similar Techniques

Certain differences in key assumptions may have contributed to some variation in the estimates from the microsimulation studies we reviewed. Variation in estimates from the studies that used other analytic approaches was likely caused in part by differences in their methodologies and the extent of their incorporation of PPACA provisions into their analyses. Variation in estimates from the employer surveys was likely due in part to differences in survey methods, respondents, and the manner in which PPACA provisions were referenced throughout the survey.

Differences in Assumptions, Time Frames of Projections, and Assessment of the Individual Mandate Likely Contributed to Small Variation in Estimates from Microsimulation Studies

Certain differences in factors, such as underlying assumptions about employer and employee decision making, may have contributed to some variation in the estimates, although the five microsimulation studies we reviewed shared methodological similarities and therefore generated relatively similar estimates of changes to employer-sponsored coverage. The studies generally used similar modeling techniques and many of the same data sets to calculate their estimates. Specifically, to construct baseline distributions of coverage in the United States and "synthetic" firms intended to reflect the demographics of employees in actual firms, the studies relied on data sets such as the Medical Expenditure Panel Survey (MEPS), the Current Population Survey (CPS), and the Survey of Income and Program Participation (SIPP).[35] The studies also made certain common assumptions. For instance, most assumed, as illustrated by evidence in the literature, that employers electing to drop coverage for their employees would increase wages in order to compensate for the loss of health benefits, and certain studies noted that the increased wages would factor in the tax exclusion of health benefits.[36] However,

---

[35] The MEPS, sponsored by the Agency for Healthcare Research and Quality within the U.S. Department of Health and Human Services, is a set of large-scale surveys of families and individuals, their medical providers, and their employers across the United States. The surveys collect data on the cost and use of health care and health coverage. The CPS is sponsored jointly by the U.S. Census Bureau and the U.S. Bureau of Labor Statistics and collects data on labor force statistics for the population of the United States, including data on employment and earnings. The SIPP is sponsored by the U.S. Census Bureau and also collects information about the labor force, including the source and amount of income and other demographic data.

[36] Experts have noted that if employers choose to stop offering health coverage to their employees, they will generally increase employees' wages to help compensate for the loss of benefits and to continue to attract a competitive workforce.

another researcher has noted that employers' decisions to increase employees' wages in lieu of offering health coverage will depend on a number of factors—most important the strength of the economy and the labor market. Further, most studies assumed that employers generally make decisions about health coverage based on their entire workforce and would not offer health benefits to some, but not all, employees. For example, CBO noted that there are legal and economic obstacles to offering health benefits to only certain employees, including a prohibition on discrimination in favor of highly compensated individuals.[37] Such similar assumptions likely contributed to the consistency of the studies' estimates, which suggested that PPACA would result in relatively small changes to employer-sponsored coverage in the near term.

However, differences in underlying assumptions about employer and employee responses to PPACA, the time frames of projections, and assessment of the effectiveness of PPACA's individual mandate likely contributed to some variation in the estimates.

- **Modeling employer and employee responses to PPACA**: The studies generally used one of two different approaches to model employer and employee responses to PPACA. The CBO study drew from available evidence in health economics literature about historical responses to premium changes in order to model the future decisions of employers and employees in response to PPACA.[38] The RAND and Urban Institute/RWJF studies assumed that employers and employees would make optimal choices by weighing the financial costs and benefits of available options, taking into account factors such as the PPACA-imposed individual and employer penalties for not

---

[37]Congressional Budget Office, *CBO and JCT's Estimates of the Effects of the Affordable Care Act on the Number of People Obtaining Employment-Based Health Insurance* (March 2012), 18 (citing 26 U.S.C. § 105(h) and 42 U.S.C. § 300gg-16 (as added by Pub. L. No. 111-148, §1001, 124 Stat. 130)).

[38]Researchers have referred to this method as an elasticity-based approach. Price elasticity is a commonly used economic tool that measures consumers' sensitivity to price changes.

obtaining or offering coverage.[39] The Lewin Group study used a combination of the two approaches.[40]

- **Time frames of the estimates**: While each microsimulation model estimated the effects of PPACA in a certain year as compared to coverage without PPACA in a given year, the models varied in their time frame of focus. The Lewin Group and Urban Institute/RWJF studies we reviewed simulated the effects of PPACA in 2011 (assuming implementation of key PPACA provisions). However, the RAND study simulated the effects of PPACA in 2016, and the CBO and CMS studies simulated the effects of PPACA over a range of years (2012 through 2022 and 2010 through 2019, respectively).[41]

- **Compliance with the individual mandate**: Models varied in their assessment of the degree of compliance with PPACA's individual mandate. The CMS and Urban Institute/RWJF studies assumed compliance would be driven by both the financial incentive of a penalty as well as the desire to obey a statutory mandate. Similarly, the CBO study assumed that compliance with the mandate would be high, even among individuals exempt from penalties, because of a natural preference for complying with the law. CBO also assumed that the penalties for noncompliance may be imperfectly enforced. However, the RAND study assumed that penalties for noncompliance would be perfectly enforced, but did not assume that the mandate

---

[39]This method was referred to as a utility maximization approach.

[40]Study authors conducted sensitivity analyses to determine how estimates would differ under alternate assumptions. For example, CBO's estimates of the number of people with employer-sponsored coverage ranged from a decrease of 20 million to an increase of 3 million compared to coverage without PPACA under varying assumptions about employers' sensitivity to the cost of health insurance and the effect of the individual mandate. CBO indicated that these alternative assumptions about employer behavior were unlikely or inconsistent with previous research. Other studies projected smaller variations in estimates because of different assumptions. Specifically, the Urban Institute/RWJF estimate ranged from a decrease of 0.81 million to a decrease of 2.1 million because of varying assumptions about the success of the exchanges, and RAND found that employer coverage was relatively insensitive to the assumptions it tested, including an employer preference for maintaining the status quo (in other words, a preference for continuing to offer coverage directly rather than through the exchanges, despite financial incentives to make this change).

[41]Because data were generally adjusted to statistically correspond to studies' years of focus—for example, data in the RAND study were "aged" to reflect projected 2016 prices—resulting estimates of coverage may differ from studies that focused on other years.

would increase compliance among individuals exempt from penalties. Similarly The Lewin Group also assumed a lower compliance with the individual mandate than CBO, in part because there are no legal consequences to going without coverage beyond the penalty.

Differences in Study Methodologies and Consideration of PPACA Provisions Likely Led to Wider Variation in Estimates from Studies Using Other Analytic Approaches

Estimates from the three studies that used other analytic approaches varied more widely likely in part because of differences in the studies' methodologies as well as their consideration of PPACA provisions. For example, the EPI study, which predicted a net increase of 4 million in the number of individuals with employer-sponsored coverage, incorporated some of the statistical modeling techniques and underlying theory of employer and employee behavior used by the microsimulation models, and was therefore able to more systematically examine the combined effects of PPACA's provisions.[42] The American Action Forum study, which predicted that up to 35 million individuals may lose employer-sponsored coverage, used a cost-benefit comparison, examining individual employers' financial trade-offs between offering coverage and dropping coverage for employees of different income levels and paying the employer penalties and increasing employees' wages to compensate. The study suggested that PPACA provides strong financial incentives for employers to drop coverage for many of their low-income employees, but that there are few incentives to drop coverage for higher-income employees. Certain researchers have noted key limitations of the study, including that it did not take into account the impact of PPACA's individual mandate, the nonfederal tax advantage of employer-sponsored coverage, the cost of single health coverage plans, and the nondiscrimination rules that may prevent employers from dropping coverage for some, but not all, employees.[43] Additionally, unlike the other two studies, this study did not measure the net effect of PPACA on employer health coverage, thus

---

[42]The purpose of this study was not to estimate the effects of PPACA per se, but rather to illustrate how these estimates might change under different assumptions about the definition of affordability of coverage and the extent of premium cost sharing between employers and employees. The study concluded that PPACA would further decrease the number of people with employer-sponsored coverage if the definition of affordability of coverage (which is currently based on single coverage) was changed to single or family coverage as applicable, and if employees were responsible for paying the entire share of premium costs.

[43]See G. Bowen and M. Buettgens, *Employer-Sponsored Insurance Under Health Reform: Reports of Its Demise Are Premature*, Urban Institute/RWJF (Washington, D.C.: 2011).

addressing only those that may drop coverage but not those that may newly offer it. Finally, the Booz and Company Inc. study, which predicted a net decrease of 3 to 4 million in the number of individuals with employer-sponsored coverage, used a combination of interviews, focus groups, surveys, and statistical modeling to derive its estimates.[44] The study estimated the change in employer-sponsored coverage between 2 years—2009 and 2016—but did not separate the effects of PPACA from any changes to employer-sponsored coverage that may occur between these years because of factors unrelated to PPACA, such as a continuation of the overall declining rates of employer-sponsored coverage since the last decade.[45]

Variation in Estimates from Employer Surveys Was Likely Due to Differences in Survey Methods and Assumptions about Respondent Knowledge of PPACA Provisions

Varying estimates from the 16 employer surveys of the extent to which employers were likely to drop health coverage may have stemmed from differences in sampling techniques, the response rates and number of respondents, the types of employers surveyed, the framing of survey questions, and the manner in which PPACA provisions were referenced throughout the survey.[46]

- **Sampling techniques and number of respondents**: Surveys varied in the methodology used to draw their sample of respondents. Some, such as the Mercer survey, sampled randomly within the national employer population, which helped ensure that results were generalizable to all nonsurveyed employers with similar characteristics. Others, such as the International Foundation of Employee Benefit Plans (IFEBP) survey, used nonrandom sampling techniques, which limited the generalizability of their results. In addition, the number of survey respondents ranged widely, from 104 in the Benfield Research survey to about 2,840 in the Mercer survey,

---

[44]We could not fully assess the methodology of this study since detailed information was not publicly available.

[45]The EPI study modeled the effects of PPACA as if key provisions were implemented in 2008. The American Action Forum study simulated employer decisions in 2014, but it was unclear whether it drew from predicted coverage levels without PPACA in 2014 or current coverage levels at the time of publication to calculate its estimate.

[46]These differences may prevent estimates from being fully comparable. Additionally, because of a lack of publicly available information on the survey instrument and methodology for many surveys, we cannot comment on their limitations in more detail.

which also could have implications for the generalizability of results.[47] The surveys generally did not publicly disclose their response rates.

- **Employer respondent type**: Surveys varied in the type of employers surveyed. Some, such as those conducted by trade groups, were limited to members of the surveying organization. Others were limited to only small or only large employers, or employers within a particular industry, or included a broader mix of small, midsize, and large employers across all types of industries. For example, the NFIB survey included only small employers with 50 or fewer employees, while the majority of respondents to the HighRoads survey were from hospitals and other health care systems. The Mercer and Willis surveys included a wider range of employer sizes and industries. Some surveys, such as the Benfield Research survey, included only self-insured employers, and others, such as the McKinsey survey, included only private sector employers.

- **Framing of the survey questions**: Surveys varied in the manner in which they asked whether employers were planning to drop health coverage in response to PPACA. For example, the Fidelity Investments (Fidelity) survey reported whether respondents were "seriously thinking about no longer offering health care coverage," the HR Policy Association survey asked if respondents were giving "serious consideration to discontinuing providing health benefits," and the NFIB survey asked if employers were "not at all likely" or "not too likely" to "have an employee insurance plan 12 months from now." In addition, some surveys reported specifically about active employee health plans, while others did not distinguish between active employees and retirees. For example, the Towers Watson survey reported whether respondents planned to "replace health care plans for active employees working 30+ hours per week with a financial subsidy" while the GfK Custom Research North America survey reported whether employers were "very or somewhat likely to drop coverage" without specifying whether this was for active employees or retirees.[48]

---

[47]Surveys with a greater number of respondents are generally considered to be more generalizable than surveys with fewer respondents.

[48]Although we considered these questions similar for the purposes of our analysis, they may elicit different responses even if presented to the same respondents.

- **Referencing of PPACA provisions**: Surveys varied in their assumptions of respondent knowledge of PPACA provisions. For example, 11 surveys assumed a certain level of respondent awareness of key PPACA provisions and did not specifically refer to the provisions in the phrasing of their questions about plans to drop coverage. However, other surveys phrased their questions in the context of specific PPACA provisions or explicitly asked respondents about their knowledge of the provisions. For example, the PricewaterhouseCoopers survey asked how likely respondents were to "cover employees through state-run health insurance exchange pools," and the Willis survey asked how likely respondents were to "drop coverage to trigger migration of employees to state-based exchanges." The McKinsey survey also phrased its questions about discontinuing health coverage in the context of select PPACA provisions and provided additional information to respondents to inform them about the provisions.[49]

---

[49]The McKinsey survey included three questions relating to employer plans for dropping or retaining coverage in light of the enhanced availability of coverage through the small business and individual market insurance exchanges. The first question, directed at respondents with 1 to 99 employees, noted the availability of Small Business Health Options Programs (SHOPs)— exchanges where small businesses may purchase health care for their employees. The respondent was then asked about the likelihood of the employer's continuing to offer or newly offering coverage assuming that "SHOPs become an easy, affordable way for small businesses to obtain coverage for their employees." The other two questions provided information about the availability of coverage through the individual exchanges, and respondents were asked: "Assume exchanges become an easy and affordable way for individuals to obtain health insurance. Given this information, how likely do you think your company would be to discontinue employee health coverage?" One researcher pointed out that these were "significant assumptions," and others have pointed out methodological flaws in McKinsey's survey design. McKinsey noted that its survey captured employer attitudes and was not intended to be a predictive economic analysis of the effect of PPACA.

Employer Surveys Suggest That PPACA May Have a Larger Effect on Small Employers and Certain Employee Populations and Prompt Some Employers to Change Benefit Designs

PPACA may affect certain types of employers or employers with certain employee populations more than all employers or employees. Some employers were considering benefit design changes.

PPACA May Affect Small Employers and Certain Types of Employees More Than Others

Four of five surveys that examined changes in the prevalence of employer-sponsored coverage by employer size indicated that a greater share of small employers (from 5 to 22 percent) were considering dropping coverage compared to large employers (from 2 to 14 percent) in these surveys.[50,51] These surveys included Fidelity (22 percent and 14 percent for small and large employers, respectively), McKinsey (9 percent and 5 percent for small and large employers, respectively), and Mercer (5 percent and 2 percent for small and large employers, respectively). One survey (Willis) did not indicate any differences between small and large employers.[52,53]

---

[50] Two of the microsimulation studies noted that small employers and those with predominantly low-wage workers would be more likely to drop employer-sponsored coverage than large employers; however, no numerical estimates were published.

[51] The definitions of "small" and "large" employers varied or were not clearly provided in these surveys.

[52] Other surveys may have included this question; however, the information was not publicly available.

[53] One survey that examined changes in coverage by employer size—McKinsey—also estimated that about 13 percent of small employers would begin, or continue, to offer coverage through the exchanges.

Surveys that examined changes in the prevalence of employer-sponsored coverage for certain types of beneficiaries indicated that these individuals could be more affected than others. Five of the nine surveys that considered the effect on retirees indicated that a higher proportion of employers were considering dropping coverage for retirees compared to all employees in these surveys—between 9 and 20 percent compared to 4 percent and 9 percent, respectively.[54,55,56] For example, Mercer indicated that 17 percent and 5 percent of employers were considering dropping coverage for new retirees and all employees, respectively, and Willis indicated that 9 percent and 5 percent of employers were considering dropping coverage for retirees and all employees, respectively. Two of the four remaining surveys (PricewaterhouseCoopers and IFEBP) indicated no differences between rates of employers dropping coverage for retirees and for all employees, and the remaining two only examined the effect of PPACA on subsets of employees, but not all employees. In addition, two surveys that examined the effect of PPACA on spouses and dependents indicated that between 12 and 15 percent of employers were considering dropping health coverage for spouses and dependents compared to a lower proportion for all employees. For example, McKinsey indicated that 15 percent and 9 percent of employers were definitely considering dropping coverage for spouses/dependents and all employees, respectively.

---

[54]The proportion of employers considering dropping coverage was slightly lower for pre-65 retirees compared to post-65 retirees in two surveys and somewhat higher for future retirees compared to current retirees in one survey.

[55]Of the remaining four surveys, two showed virtually no difference in rates of employers dropping coverage for retirees and other types of employees, and the remaining two examined rates for retirees but not all employees.

[56]The microsimulation studies focused on active employees and their dependents, and did not examine the effect of PPACA on retirees.

PPACA May Also Prompt Employers to Change Health Plan Benefit Design

Several of the 19 employer surveys that we reviewed also indicated that PPACA may prompt employers to consider key changes to benefit designs that will generally result in greater employee cost for health insurance.[57]

- **Increased employee cost sharing**: The 9 surveys that examined benefit design changes indicated that from 16 to 73 percent of employers were considering increasing employees' share of the cost of coverage, for example, through increased premiums, deductibles, or co-payments. For example, the IFEBP survey indicated that about 40 percent of employers had increased or were planning to increase employee premium sharing, and about 29 percent had increased or planned on increasing in-network deductibles. Similarly, the PricewaterhouseCoopers survey indicated that 61 percent planned to increase employee premium sharing, and 57 percent planned to increase employee cost sharing through other benefit design changes.

  In addition, the 7 surveys that examined employer responses to the high-cost excise tax effective under PPACA in 2018 indicated that from 11 to 88 percent of employers had plans to take steps to avoid paying the tax; in 5 of these surveys, employers planned to redesign benefits and in 2 surveys employers had not identified specific strategies but planned to take steps. For example, the Aon-Hewitt survey indicated that 25 percent of employers anticipated changing their benefits to reduce plan cost, while the Willis survey indicated that 22 percent planned to increase deductibles or co-payments to avoid the tax.

- **Use of account-based plans**: The 9 surveys that examined employer plans to offer account based plans, such as high-deductible health plans (HDHP), consumer-directed health plans (CDHP), or health savings accounts indicated that from 17 to 73 percent of employers either had plans to offer such plans or saw the plans as attractive options for providing health coverage. For example, the Benfield Research survey indicated that about two-thirds of employers planned

---

[57]Several trends in employer-sponsored coverage predate PPACA, including increases in the employee share of health plan premiums and cost sharing and increases in the prevalence of account-based health plans. See Kaiser Family Foundation and HRET, *2011 Annual Survey*.

to offer a CDHP by 2015, and the Towers Watson survey indicated that 17 percent planned to start offering HDHPs in 2013 or 2014, bringing the total share of employers with HDHPs up to 74 percent.

- **Move to self-insurance**: Two of the 3 surveys that examined employers potentially becoming self-insured in response to PPACA indicated that from 12 to 52 percent were considering doing so, and the remaining survey indicated that 13 percent of employers reported increasing their consideration of such a move in response to PPACA.[58] For example, the IFEBP survey indicated that about 52 percent of employers were considering such a move, compared to only about 6 percent in a prior year's survey.

External Comments

We provided a draft of this report to two researchers with expertise in employee health benefits issues. They agreed with our report and provided suggestions and technical comments, which we incorporated as appropriate.

As agreed with your office, unless you publicly announce the contents of this report earlier, we plan no further distribution until 30 days from the report date. At that time, we will send a copy to the Secretary of Health and Human Services. In addition, the report will be available at no charge on the GAO website at http://www.gao.gov.

---

[58]Self-insured employee health benefit plans are not subject to state insurance regulations or to certain requirements in PPACA that apply to fully insured plans—for example, required coverage of certain "essential" health benefits. See 29 U.S.C. § 1144 (certain employee benefit plans not subject to state laws); 42 U.S.C. §§ 18021, 18022 (as added by Pub. L. No. 111-148, §§ 1301, 1302, 124 Stat. 162,163) (certain employee benefit plans excluded from definition of "health plan" and requirement to provide essential health benefits under PPACA). Some researchers have raised concerns that employers with healthier employees are more likely to become self-insured, thereby leaving the exchanges—particularly for the small group market—with relatively sicker enrollees, and thereby driving up premiums in the exchanges.

If you or your staff have any questions about this report, please contact me at (202) 512-7114 or dickenj@gao.gov. Contact points for our Offices of Congressional Relations and Public Affairs may be found on the last page of this report. GAO staff who made key contributions to this report are listed in appendix II.

Sincerely yours,

John E. Dicken
Director, Health Care

Appendix I: Studies Reviewed by GAO

We reviewed the 27 studies listed below that contained original numerical estimates of the effect of the Patient Protection and Affordable Care Act (PPACA) on the prevalence of employer-sponsored coverage[1]—5 based on microsimulation models,[2] 3 based on other analytic approaches, and 19 based on employer surveys.[3]

Microsimulation Models

1. Centers for Medicare & Medicaid Services.

    Foster, R. S., Centers for Medicare & Medicaid Services Office of the Actuary. *Estimated Financial Effects of the "Patient Protection and Affordable Care Act,"* as Amended. Baltimore, Md.: April 2010.

2. Congressional Budget Office (CBO).

    CBO and JCT's Estimates of the Effects of the Affordable Care Act on the Number of People Obtaining Employment-Based Health Insurance. Washington, D.C.: March 2012.

    Updated Estimates for the Insurance Coverage Provisions of the Affordable Care Act. Washington, D.C.: March 2012.

    Banthin, J. *Effects of Eliminating the Individual Mandate to Obtain Health Insurance.* Presentation at Bloomberg Government/Rand Corporation event. Washington, D.C.: March 2012.

    Elmendorf, D. W. *CBO's Analysis of the Major Health Care Legislation Enacted in March 2010.* Testimony before the Subcommittee on Health, Committee on Energy and Commerce, House of Representatives. Washington, D.C.: March 2011.

---

[1] We reviewed studies published from January 1, 2009, through March 30, 2012, that provided an original numerical estimate at the national level of the prevalence of, or changes to, rates of employer-sponsored coverage.

[2] Multiple microsimulation studies conducted by the same organization were counted as one study for our purposes because they used the same proprietary microsimulation model.

[3] Employer surveys conducted by the same firm in multiple years were counted as one study for our purposes because the newer surveys generally updated relevant findings from the previous surveys. The full text of certain surveys was not publicly available; in these cases, we cite the press releases we reviewed that contained the surveys' findings.

Appendix I: Studies Reviewed by GAO

H.R. 4872, Reconciliation Act of 2010 (Final Health Care Legislation). Washington, D.C.: March 2010.

3. The Lewin Group.

   Sheils, J. F. and R. Haught. "Without the Individual Mandate, the Affordable Care Act Would Still Cover 23 Million; Premiums Would Rise Less Than Predicted." *Health Affairs*, vol. 30, no. 11 (2011).[4]

   Patient Protection and Affordable Care Act (PPACA): Long Term Costs for Governments, Employers, Families and Providers. Staff Working Paper # 11. Falls Church, Va.: 2010.

4. RAND Corporation.

   Eibner, C. and C. C. Price. *The Effect of the Affordable Care Act on Enrollment and Premiums, With and Without the Individual Mandate.* Santa Monica, Calif.: 2012.

   Eibner, C. et al. *Establishing State Health Insurance Exchanges: Implications for Health Insurance Enrollment, Spending, and Small Business.* Santa Monica, Calif.: 2010.

5. The Urban Institute/Robert Wood Johnson Foundation.

   Buettgens, M. and C. Carroll. *Eliminating the Individual Mandate: Effects on Premiums Coverage, and Uncompensated Care.* Washington, D.C., and Princeton, N.J.: January 2012.

   Garrett, B. and M. Buettgens. *Employer-Sponsored Insurance under Health Reform: Reports of Its Demise Are Premature.* Washington, D.C., and Princeton, N.J.: January 2011.

---

[4]The authors of this study are staff members of The Lewin Group, and the study was conducted using The Lewin Group's proprietary microsimulation model. We therefore consider it to be a study by The Lewin Group for our purposes.

Appendix I: Studies Reviewed by GAO

Other Analytic Approaches

6. Ahlquist, G. D., P. F. Borromeo, and S. B. Saxena. *The Future of Health Insurance: Demise of Employer-Sponsored Coverage Greatly Exaggerated*. Booz & Company Inc. 2011.

7. Burkhauser, R. V., S. Lyons, and K. Simon. *An Offer You Can't Refuse: Estimating the Coverage Efffects of the 2010 Affordable Care Act*. Washington, D.C.: Employment Policies Institute, July 2011.

   Burkhauser, R. V., S. Lyons, and K. Simon. *The Importance of the Meaning and Measurement of "Affordable" in the Affordable Care Act*. Working Paper # 17279, National Bureau of Economic Research. Cambridge, Mass.: August 2011.

8. Holtz-Eakin, D. and C. Smith. Labor Markets and Health Care Reform: New Results. American Action Forum. Washington, D.C.: May 2010.

Employer Surveys

9. Aon Hewitt. *Employer Reaction to Health Care Reform: Retiree Strategy Survey*. Lincolnshire, Ill.: 2011.

10. Benfield Research. *Special Report: Employer Market Healthcare Reform Research Summary*. St. Louis, Mo.: 2011.

11. Ceridian Health Care Compass. "Health Care Reform Presents New Challenges, Choices to U.S. Employers." Issue 21. Cites findings from Ceridian's Health Care Compass reader poll, July 2011. Accessed February 1, 2012. http://www.ceridian.com/employee_benefits_article/1,6266,15766-79463,00.html.

12. Fidelity Investments. *Fidelity Investments Survey Finds Majority of Employers Rethinking Health Care Strategy Post Health Care Reform*. Boston, Mass.: July 2010. Accessed March 6, 2012. http://www.fidelity.com/inside-fidelity/employer-services/fidelity-survey-finds-majority-of-employers-rethinking-health-care-strategy-post-health-care-reform.

13. GfK Custom Research North America. *Employers Skeptical of Health Reform, But Few Project Dropping Health Insurance Coverage."* New York, N.Y.: December 2011. Accessed March 29, 2012. http://www.gfkamerica.com/newsroom/press_releases/single_sites/009103/index.en.html.

Appendix I: Studies Reviewed by GAO

14. HighRoads. "HighRoads Study Shows Employers Will Not Eliminate Benefits Coverage Due to Health Care Reform." December 2011. Accessed February 1, 2012. http://newsroom.highroads.com/hr-compliance-connection/highroads-study-shows-employers-will-not-eliminate-benefits-coverage-due-to-health-care-reform.

15. HR Policy Association.

    2011 Annual Chief Human Resource Officer Survey. Washington, D.C.

    2010 Summer Chief Human Resource Officer Survey: Questions on the New Health Care Law. Washington, D.C.

16. International Foundation of Employee Benefit Plans.

    Health Care Reform: Employer Actions One Year Later; Survey Results: May 2011. Brookfield, Wis.: 2011.

    Health Care Reform: What Employers Are Considering; Survey Results: May 2010. Brookfield, Wis.: 2010.

17. Kaiser Family Foundation and Health Research & Education Trust. *Employer Health Benefits 2011 Annual Survey*. Menlo Park, Calif., and Chicago, Ill.: September 2011.

18. Lockton Companies, LLC. *Employer Health Reform Survey Results, June 2011*. Kansas City, Mo.: 2011.

19. Market Strategies International. *Many Companies Intend to Drop Employer Coverage in 2014 as Health Care Reform Takes Full Effect*. Livonia, Mich.: January 2011. Accessed May 1, 2012. http://www.marketstrategies.com/news/1902/1/Many-Companies-Intend-to-Drop-Employee-Coverage-in-2014-as-Health-Care-Reform-Takes-Full-Effect.aspx.

20. McKinsey & Company. *How US Health Care Reform Will Affect Employee Benefits*. 2011.

Appendix I: Studies Reviewed by GAO

21. Mercer, LLC.

    National Survey of Employer-Sponsored Health Plans: 2011 Survey Report. New York, N.Y.: 2012.

    National Survey of Employer-Sponsored Health Plans: 2010 Survey Report. New York, N.Y.: 2011.

22. Midwest Business Group on Health. Financial Impact of Health Reform on Employer Benefits Not as Significant as Anticipated. Chicago, Ill.: March 2012. Accessed March 29, 2012. http://www.mbgh.org/mbgh/news/2012pressreleases/go.aspx?navigationkey=a4956928-cca2-495a-94fc-ed56ce991fcd.

23. National Business Group on Health.

    Large Employers' 2011 Health Plan Design Changes. Washington, D.C.: 2010.

    Majority of Employers Revamping Health Benefit Programs for 2012, National Business Group on Health Survey Finds. Washington, D.C.: August 2011. Accessed January 1, 2012. http://www.wbgh.org/pressrelease.cfm?ID=179.

24. National Federation of Independent Business. *Small Business and Health Insurance: One Year After Enactment of PPACA*. Washington, D.C.: 2011.

25. PricewaterhouseCoopers LLP. *Health and Well-Being Touchstone Survey Results, May 2011*. New York, N.Y.: May 2011.

26. Towers Watson.

    Health Care Changes Ahead: Survey Report. New York, N.Y.: October 2011.

    Health Care Reform: Looming Fears Mask Unprecedented Employer Opportunities To Mitigate Costs, Risk, and Reset Total Rewards. New York, N.Y.: May 2010.

Appendix I: Studies Reviewed by GAO

27. Willis Group Holdings plc.

Willis. *The Health Care Reform Survey, 2011-2012.* New York, N.Y.: 2011-2012.

Diamond Management Technology Consultants and Willis North America. *The Health Care Reform Survey, 2010.* New York, N.Y.: 2010.

Appendix II: GAO Contact and Staff Acknowledgments

GAO Contact	John E. Dicken, (202) 512-7114 or dickenj@gao.gov
Staff Acknowledgments	In addition to the contact named above, Randy DiRosa (Assistant Director), Iola D'Souza, Yesook Merrill, Laurie Pachter, and Priyanka Sethi made key contributions to this report.

GAO's Mission	The Government Accountability Office, the audit, evaluation, and investigative arm of Congress, exists to support Congress in meeting its constitutional responsibilities and to help improve the performance and accountability of the federal government for the American people. GAO examines the use of public funds; evaluates federal programs and policies; and provides analyses, recommendations, and other assistance to help Congress make informed oversight, policy, and funding decisions. GAO's commitment to good government is reflected in its core values of accountability, integrity, and reliability.
Obtaining Copies of GAO Reports and Testimony	The fastest and easiest way to obtain copies of GAO documents at no cost is through GAO's website (www.gao.gov). Each weekday afternoon, GAO posts on its website newly released reports, testimony, and correspondence. To have GAO e-mail you a list of newly posted products, go to www.gao.gov and select "E-mail Updates."
Order by Phone	The price of each GAO publication reflects GAO's actual cost of production and distribution and depends on the number of pages in the publication and whether the publication is printed in color or black and white. Pricing and ordering information is posted on GAO's website, http://www.gao.gov/ordering.htm. Place orders by calling (202) 512-6000, toll free (866) 801-7077, or TDD (202) 512-2537. Orders may be paid for using American Express, Discover Card, MasterCard, Visa, check, or money order. Call for additional information.
Connect with GAO	Connect with GAO on Facebook, Flickr, Twitter, and YouTube. Subscribe to our RSS Feeds or E-mail Updates. Listen to our Podcasts. Visit GAO on the web at www.gao.gov.
To Report Fraud, Waste, and Abuse in Federal Programs	Contact: Website: www.gao.gov/fraudnet/fraudnet.htm E-mail: fraudnet@gao.gov Automated answering system: (800) 424-5454 or (202) 512-7470
Congressional Relations	Katherine Siggerud, Managing Director, siggerudk@gao.gov, (202) 512-4400, U.S. Government Accountability Office, 441 G Street NW, Room 7125, Washington, DC 20548
Public Affairs	Chuck Young, Managing Director, youngc1@gao.gov, (202) 512-4800 U.S. Government Accountability Office, 441 G Street NW, Room 7149 Washington, DC 20548

Please Print on Recycled Paper.

www.ingramcontent.com/pod-product-compliance
Lightning Source LLC
Chambersburg PA
CBHW081802170526
45167CB00008B/3288